12/25/93

A few minutes each day to reflect on God's love. ❧

Presented to

Mark McGuire

From

Judy, Richard & Adam

❧

Under the Shepherd's Care

Under the Shepherd's Care

Charles L. Allen
& Mildred F. Parker

Fleming H. Revell Company
Tarrytown, New York

This is the day which the Lord hath made; we will rejoice and be glad in it.

Psalm 118:24 (KJV)

Under the Shepherd's Care

❦

January

The Twenty-third Psalm can do marvelous things for any person. Its power lies in the fact that it represents a positive, hopeful, faith approach to life. It does not begin with a petition asking God for something, rather it is a calm statement of fact—"The Lord is my shepherd; I shall not want." We do not have to beg God for things.

Instinctively, the sheep knows the shepherd made ample provision for it today, so will he tomorrow. All life came from God. That includes my life. God keeps faith with fowls of the air and the grass of the field. And Jesus asks us to think that if God will do so much for a simple bird or a wildflower, how much more will He do for us (Matthew 6:26 KJV).

Saint Paul says, "My God shall supply all your need" (Philippians 4:19 KJV). David put it, "The Lord is my shepherd; I shall not want." With that faith we can work today without worrying about tomorrow.

❦

January 1

From the fullness of his grace we have all received one blessing after another.

John 1:16 (NIV)

Blessings God has given me:

_____

_____

_____

January 2

In the Lord have I righteousness and strength.

Isaiah 45:24 (KJV)

My prayer concerns are:

_____

_____

_____

_____

January 3

It is because of him that you are in Christ Jesus, who has become for us wisdom from God—that is, our righteousness, holiness and redemption.
                                 1 Corinthians 1:30 (NIV)

What this verse means to me:

_____

_____

_____

January 4

Godliness with contentment is great gain.
                                 1 Timothy 6:6 (KJV)

Promises I claim today:

_____

_____

_____

❦

January 5

Whoever does not receive the kingdom of God like a child shall not enter it.

Mark 10:15 (RSV)

Who needs my love today:

_____

_____

_____

January 6

It is an honour for a man to cease from strife.

Proverbs 20:3 (KJV)

Things that remind me of God's greatness:

_____

_____

_____

_____

January 7

Fear thou not; for I am with thee: be not dismayed; for I am thy God: I will strengthen thee; yea, I will help thee.

Isaiah 41:10 (KJV)

Today I thank God for:

_____

_____

_____

January 8

The Lord is with you when you are with him. If you seek him, he will be found by you.

2 Chronicles 15:2 (NIV)

People I am remembering this week:

_____

_____

_____

January 9

The Lord, he it is that doth go before thee; he will be with thee, he will not fail thee, neither forsake thee.

Deuteronomy 31:8 (KJV)

How I can claim this blessing today:

_____

_____

_____

January 10

Blessed is the people that know the joyful sound: they shall walk, O Lord, in the light of thy countenance. In thy name shall they rejoice all the day: and in thy righteousness shall they be exalted.

Psalm 89:15, 16 (KJV)

Today I am praying for:

_____

_____

❧

January 11

Thou shalt be stedfast, and shalt not fear.

Job 11:15 (KJV)

How I can put this verse into action today:

_____

_____

_____

January 12

Be of good courage, and he shall strengthen your heart, all ye that hope in the Lord.

Psalm 31:24 (KJV)

Things that remind me of God's goodness:

_____

_____

_____

_____

January 13

The Lord giveth wisdom: out of his mouth cometh knowledge and understanding. He layeth up sound wisdom for the righteous.

Proverbs 2:6, 7 (KJV)

Blessings God has given me:

_____

_____

_____

January 14

I will instruct thee and teach thee in the way which thou shalt go: I will guide thee with mine eye.

Psalm 32:8 (KJV)

My prayer concerns are:

_____

_____

_____

January 15

And whenever you stand praying, forgive, if you have anything against any one; so that your Father also who is in heaven may forgive you your trespasses.

Mark 11:25 (RSV)

What this verse means to me:

_____

_____

_____

January 16

Blessed are the merciful, for they will be shown mercy.

Matthew 5:7 (NIV)

Promises I claim today:

_____

_____

_____

❦

January 17

Love your enemies, bless them that curse you, do good to them that hate you, and pray for them which despitefully use you, and persecute you.

Matthew 5:44 (KJV)

Who needs my love today:

_____

_____

_____

January 18

For if you forgive men when they sin against you, your heavenly Father will also forgive you.

Matthew 6:14 (NIV)

Things that remind me of God's greatness:

_____

_____

_____

January 19

And it shall come to pass, that before they call,
I will answer; and while they are yet speaking,
I will hear.

Isaiah 65:24 (KJV)

Today I thank God for:

_____

_____

_____

January 20

Then shalt thou call, and the Lord shall answer;
thou shalt cry, and he shall say, Here I am.

Isaiah 58:9 (KJV)

People I am remembering this week:

_____

_____

_____

January 21

Ask, and it will be given you; seek, and you will find; knock, and it will be opened to you. For every one who asks receives, and he who seeks finds, and to him who knocks it will be opened.

Matthew 7:7, 8 (RSV)

How I can claim this blessing today:

_____

_____

_____

January 22

God was pleased . . . to save those who believe.

1 Corinthians 1:21 (NIV)

Today I am praying for:

_____

_____

_____

January 23

Faith comes from hearing the message, and the message is heard through the word of Christ.

Romans 10:17 (NIV)

How I can put this verse into action today:

January 24

I have complete confidence in the gospel; it is God's power to save all who believe.

Romans 1:16 (TEV)

Things that remind me of God's goodness:

January 25

Anything you did for one of my brothers here, however humble, you did for me.

Matthew 25:40 (NEB)

Blessings God has given me:

_____

_____

_____

January 26

This God is our God for ever and ever: he will be our guide even unto death.

Psalm 48:14 (KJV)

My prayer concerns are:

_____

_____

_____

_____

January 27

When anyone is joined to Christ he is a new
being; the old is gone, the new has come.

2 Corinthians 5:17 (TEV)

What this verse means to me:

_____

_____

_____

January 28

That the God of our Lord Jesus Christ, the all-
glorious Father, may give you the spiritual pow-
ers of wisdom and vision, by which there comes
the knowledge of him.

Ephesians 1:17 (NEB)

Promises I claim today:

_____

_____

_____

January 29

And we have seen and testify that the Father has sent his Son to be the Savior of the world.

1 John 4:14 (NIV)

Who needs my love today:

_____

_____

_____

January 30

Wherefore seeing we also are compassed about with so great a cloud of witnesses, let us lay aside every weight, and the sin which doth so easily beset us, and let us run with patience the race that is set before us.

Hebrews 12:1 (KJV)

Things that remind me of God's greatness:

_____

_____

January 31

In Christ Jesus the life-giving law of the Spirit has set you free from the law of sin and death.

Romans 8:2 (NEB)

Today I thank God for:

_____

_____

_____

❦

February

The Psalmist says, "Delight thyself also in the Lord; and he shall give thee the desires of thine heart." But to fail to become molded or controlled by God's will is to destroy ourselves.

There are times when, with our limited vision, it seems that God's way is not the best way. We want material success on earth, we want happiness in our lives and peace in our hearts. If we believed, really believed, God would give us what we so much want; we would gladly be meek, that is, be willing to be molded and controlled by God.

It was not until he became an old man that Job knew without doubt that God is never defeated. How wonderful it is to learn that lesson while there is still much of life to be lived. The very act of accepting the will of God for your life today places the responsibility of what happens tomorrow on God. So do not worry about what the result will be. There is wonderful peace in leaving the results in His hands.

❦

February 1

This is a true saying, to be completely accepted and believed: Christ Jesus came into the world to save sinners.

1 Timothy 1:15 (TEV)

People I am remembering this week:

_____

_____

_____

February 2

He was wounded for our transgressions, he was bruised for our iniquities: the chastisement of our peace was upon him; and with his stripes we are healed.

Isaiah 53:5 (KJV)

How I can claim this blessing today:

_____

_____

❧

February 3

If you keep my commandments, you will abide in my love.

John 15:10 (RSV)

Today I am praying for:

_____

_____

_____

February 4

Lord, who shall abide in thy tabernacle? who shall dwell in thy holy hill? He that walketh uprightly, and worketh righteousness.

Psalm 15:1, 2 (KJV)

How I can put this verse into action today:

_____

_____

_____

❧

February 5

The prayer of the upright is his delight.

Proverbs 15:8 (KJV)

Things that remind me of God's goodness:

_____

_____

_____

February 6

Wait on the Lord: be of good courage, and he shall strengthen thy heart: wait, I say, on the Lord.

Psalm 27:14 (KJV)

Blessings God has given me:

_____

_____

_____

February 7

The Lord is my rock, and my fortress, and my deliverer; my God, my strength, in whom I will trust; my buckler, and the horn of my salvation, and my high tower.

Psalm 18:2 (KJV)

My prayer concerns are:

_____

_____

_____

February 8

God is our refuge and strength, a very present help in trouble.

Psalm 46:1 (KJV)

What this verse means to me:

_____

_____

February 9

Your sons and your daughters shall prophesy,
your old men shall dream dreams, your young
men shall see visions.

Joel 2:28 (KJV)

Promises I claim today:

_____

_____

_____

February 10

Why art thou cast down, O my soul? and why
art thou disquieted within me? hope thou in
God: for I shall yet praise him, who is the health
of my countenance, and my God.

Psalm 42:11 (KJV)

Who needs my love today:

_____

_____

February 11

"Happy are the dead who from now on die in the service of the Lord!" "Certainly so," answers the Spirit. "They will enjoy rest from their hard work, because the results of their service go with them."

Revelation 14:13 (TEV)

Things that remind me of God's greatness:

_____

_____

_____

February 12

The name of the Lord is a strong tower: the righteous runneth into it, and is safe.

Proverbs 18:10 (KJV)

Today I thank God for:

_____

_____

February 13

I will both lay me down in peace, and sleep: for thou, Lord, only makest me dwell in safety.

Psalm 4:8 (KJV)

People I am remembering this week:

_____

_____

_____

February 14

I have set the Lord always before me: because he is at my right hand, I shall not be moved.

Psalm 16:8 (KJV)

How I can claim this blessing today:

_____

_____

_____

❧

February 15

Truly, truly, I say to you, he who believes has eternal life.

John 6:47 (RSV)

Today I am praying for:

_____

_____

_____

February 16

I have been young, and now am old; yet have I not seen the righteous forsaken, nor his seed begging bread.

Psalm 37:25 (KJV)

How I can put this verse into action today:

_____

_____

_____

February 17

My own sheep listen to my voice; I know them and they follow me. I give them eternal life and they shall never perish.

John 10:27, 28 (NEB)

Things that remind me of God's goodness:

_____

_____

February 18

So that, having been justified by his grace, we might become heirs having the hope of eternal life.

Titus 3:7 (NIV)

Blessings God has given me:

_____

_____

❧

February 19

For the Lord God will help me; therefore shall I not be confounded: therefore have I set my face like a flint, and I know that I shall not be ashamed.

Isaiah 50:7 (KJV)

My prayer concerns are:

February 20

But the wisdom from above is pure, first of all; it is also peaceful, gentle, and friendly; it is full of compassion and produces a harvest of good deeds; it is free from prejudice and hypocrisy.

James 3:17 (TEV)

What this verse means to me:

February 21

There is laid up for me a crown of righteousness, which the Lord, the righteous judge, shall give me at that day: and not to me only, but unto all them also that love his appearing.

2 Timothy 4:8 (KJV)

Promises I claim today:

_____

_____

_____

February 22

According to his promise we wait for new heavens and a new earth in which righteousness dwells.

2 Peter 3:13 (RSV)

Who needs my love today:

_____

_____

February 23

There are many rooms in my Father's house, and I am going to prepare a place for you. I would not tell you this if it were not so.

John 14:2 (TEV)

Things that remind me of God's greatness:

_____

_____

_____

February 24

But seek first his kingdom and his righteousness, and all these things will be given to you as well.

Matthew 6:33 (NIV)

Today I thank God for:

_____

_____

February 25

And my God will supply every need of yours
according to his riches in glory in Christ Jesus.
Philippians 4:19 (RSV)

People I am remembering this week:

_____

_____

_____

February 26

Whom the Lord loveth he correcteth; even as a
father the son in whom he delighteth.
Proverbs 3:12 (KJV)

How I can claim this blessing today:

_____

_____

_____

❦

February 27

Thou shalt rejoice in the Lord, and shalt glory in
the Holy One of Israel.

Isaiah 41:16 (KJV)

Today I am praying for:

_____

_____

_____

February 28

Our heart shall rejoice in him, because we have
trusted in his holy name.

Psalm 33:21 (KJV)

How I can put this verse into action today:

_____

_____

_____

❧

February 29

In God I trust; I will not be afraid. What can man do to me?

Psalm 56:11 (NIV)

How I can claim this blessing today:

_____

_____

_____

❧

❧

March

God knows our limitations, and He does not condemn us because we have weaknesses. He does not force us where we cannot safely and happily go. God never demands of us work which is beyond our strength and abilities. Instead, God is constantly ministering to our needs. He understands the loads upon our shoulders.

We are told, "He will not suffer thy foot to be moved: he that keepeth thee will not slumber. Behold, he that keepeth Israel shall neither slumber nor sleep" (Psalm 121:3, 4 KJV). It gives us confidence to know that even while we are sleeping, the Shepherd is working to prepare for our needs tomorrow.

❧

March 1

I shall see you again, and then you will be joyful, and no one shall rob you of your joy.
                                                    John 16:22 (NEB)

Things that remind me of God's goodness:

_____

_____

_____

March 2

I have the strength to face all conditions by the power that Christ gives me.
                                                    Philippians 4:13 (TEV)

Blessings God has given me:

_____

_____

_____

❦

March 3

No, in all these things we are more than conquerors through him who loved us.

Romans 8:37 (RSV)

My prayer concerns are:

_____

_____

_____

March 4

Therefore I tell you, whatever you ask for in prayer, believe that you have received it, and it will be yours.

Mark 11:24 (NIV)

What this verse means to me:

_____

_____

_____

❧

March 5

The Lord is my light and my salvation; whom
shall I fear? the Lord is the strength of my life;
of whom shall I be afraid?

Psalm 27:1 (KJV)

Promises I claim today:

_____

_____

_____

March 6

Blessed be the God and Father of our Lord Jesus
Christ! By his great mercy we have been born
anew to a living hope through the resurrection
of Jesus Christ from the dead.

1 Peter 1:3 (RSV)

Who needs my love today:

_____

_____

March 7

But the fruit of the Spirit is love, joy, peace, longsuffering, gentleness, goodness, faith, meekness, temperance: against such there is no law.

Galatians 5:22, 23 (KJV)

Things that remind me of God's greatness:

―――――――――――――――――

―――――――――――――――――

―――――――――――――――――

March 8

Whoever loves me will obey my message. My Father will love him, and my Father and I will come to him and live with him.

John 14:23 (TEV)

Today I thank God for:

―――――――――――――――――

―――――――――――――――――

March 9

He will love thee, and bless thee, and multiply thee.

Deuteronomy 7:13 (KJV)

People I am remembering this week:

_____

_____

_____

March 10

He loveth him that followeth after righteousness.

Proverbs 15:9 (KJV)

How I can claim this blessing today:

_____

_____

_____

❧

March 11

If on your lips is the confession, "Jesus is Lord",
and in your heart the faith that God raised him
from the dead, then you will find salvation.

Romans 10:9 (NEB)

Today I am praying for:

_____

_____

_____

March 12

The Son of Man came to seek and to save what
was lost.

Luke 19:10 (NIV)

How I can put this verse into action today:

_____

_____

_____

❧

March 13

I will have mercy on their transgressions, and will no longer remember their sins.

Hebrews 8:12 (TEV)

Things that remind me of God's goodness:

_____

_____

_____

March 14

And the Lord shall guide thee continually.

Isaiah 58:11 (KJV)

Blessings God has given me:

_____

_____

_____

_____

March 15

He restoreth my soul: he leadeth me in the paths
of righteousness for his name's sake.

Psalm 23:3 (KJV)

My prayer concerns are:

_____

_____

_____

March 16

The mouth of the just bringeth forth wisdom. . .
The lips of the righteous know what is accept-
able.

Proverbs 10:31, 32 (KJV)

What this verse means to me:

_____

_____

_____

March 17

The earth shall be full of the knowledge of the Lord, as the waters cover the sea.

Isaiah 11:9 (KJV)

Promises I claim today:

_____

_____

_____

March 18

And I will walk among you, and will be your God, and ye shall be my people.

Leviticus 26:12 (KJV)

Who needs my love today:

_____

_____

_____

March 19

My flesh and my heart faileth: but God is the
strength of my heart, and my portion for ever.
Psalm 73:26 (KJV)
Things that remind me of God's greatness:

_____

_____

_____

March 20

For God is not a God of confusion but of peace.
1 Corinthians 14:33 (RSV)
Today I thank God for:

_____

_____

_____

_____

March 21

The Lord God is a sun and shield: the Lord will give grace and glory: no good thing will he withhold from them that walk uprightly.

Psalm 84:11 (KJV)

People I am remembering this week:

_____

_____

_____

March 22

But now that you have been set free from sin and have become slaves to God, the benefit you reap leads to holiness, and the result is eternal life.

Romans 6:22 (NIV)

How I can claim this blessing today:

_____

_____

❧

March 23

What no man ever saw or heard, what no man ever thought could happen, is the very thing God prepared for those who love him.

1 Corinthians 2:9 (TEV)

Today I am praying for:

_____

_____

_____

March 24

You have been faithful over a little, I will set you over much; enter into the joy of your master.

Matthew 25:21 (RSV)

How I can put this verse into action today:

_____

_____

_____

☙

March 25

I have strength for anything through him who gives me power.

Philippians 4:13 (NEB)

Things that remind me of God's goodness:

_____

_____

_____

March 26

Confess your sins to each other and pray for each other so that you may be healed. The prayer of a righteous man is powerful and effective.

James 5:16 (NIV)

Blessings God has given me:

_____

_____

March 27

May the God of peace himself sanctify you wholly; and may your spirit and soul and body be kept sound and blameless at the coming of our Lord Jesus Christ.

1 Thessalonians 5:23 (RSV)

My prayer concerns are:

_____

_____

_____

March 28

Beloved, I wish above all things that thou mayest prosper and be in health, even as thy soul prospereth.

3 John 2 (KJV)

What this verse means to me:

_____

_____

March 29

The Lord is nigh unto them that are of a broken heart; and saveth such as be of a contrite spirit.

Psalm 34:18 (KJV)

Promises I claim today:

_____

_____

_____

March 30

Blessed are the poor in spirit, for theirs is the kingdom of heaven. Blessed are those who mourn, for they shall be comforted.

Matthew 5:3, 4 (RSV)

Who needs my love today:

_____

_____

_____

March 31

He who finds his life will lose it, and he who loses his life for my sake will find it.

Matthew 10:39 (RSV)

Things that remind me of God's greatness:

_____

_____

_____

❧

❧

April

Every morning the sun rises to warm the earth. If it were to fail to shine for just one minute, all life on the earth would die. The rains come to water the earth. There is fertility in the soil, life in the seeds, oxygen in the air. The providence of God is about us in unbelievable abundance every moment.

The same is true of everything you have. All of those things come from the earth which God made. He put those things within our reach because He knew we would want them and would enjoy them. Long before you were born, God answered your prayer for material blessings.

If today we would begin being thankful for what we have, and use it as best we can, God would give us insight as to how we could multiply what we have to cover every need of our lives, and have a lot left over. We would be so blessed that we would fall before Him as our Lord and King.

❧

April 1

God was in Christ, reconciling the world unto himself.

2 Corinthians 5:19 (KJV)

Today I thank God for:

_____

_____

_____

April 2

But now, O Lord, thou art our father; we are the clay, and thou our potter; and we all are the work of thy hand.

Isaiah 64:8 (KJV)

People I am remembering this week:

_____

_____

_____

April 3

I will be your father, and you shall be my sons and daughters, says the Lord Almighty.

2 Corinthians 6:18 (TEV)

How I can claim this blessing today:

_____

_____

_____

April 4

The mercy of the Lord is from everlasting to everlasting upon them that fear him, and his righteousness unto children's children; to such as keep his covenant, and to those that remember his commandments to do them.

Psalm 103:17, 18 (KJV)

Today I am praying for:

_____

_____

April 5

His delight is in the law of the Lord; and in his law doth he meditate day and night. And he shall be like a tree planted by the rivers of water, that bringeth forth his fruit in his season; his leaf also shall not wither; and whatsoever he doeth shall prosper.

Psalm 1:2, 3 (KJV)

How I can put this verse into action today:

_____

_____

April 6

This is how God showed his love among us: He sent his one and only Son into the world that we might live through him.

1 John 4:9 (NIV)

Things that remind me of God's goodness:

_____

_____

❧

April 7

Blessed is he that considereth the poor: the Lord will deliver him in time of trouble.

Psalm 41:1 (KJV)

Blessings God has given me:

_____

_____

_____

April 8

For the man who has will be given more, till he has enough and to spare.

Matthew 13:12 (NEB)

My prayer concerns are:

_____

_____

_____

❧

April 9

But the Lord is faithful; he will strengthen you
and guard you from evil.

2 Thessalonians 3:3 (RSV)

What this verse means to me:

_____

_____

_____

April 10

We know that in all things God works for good
with those who love him, those whom he has
called according to his purpose.

Romans 8:28 (TEV)

Promises I claim today:

_____

_____

_____

April 11

Delight thyself also in the Lord; and he shall give thee the desires of thine heart.

Psalm 37:4 (KJV)

Who needs my love today:

_____

_____

_____

April 12

Every word of God is pure: he is a shield unto them that put their trust in him.

Proverbs 30:5 (KJV)

Things that remind me of God's greatness:

_____

_____

_____

❧

April 13

My people shall dwell in a peaceable habitation, and in sure dwellings, and in quiet resting places.

Isaiah 32:18 (KJV)

Today I thank God for:

_____

_____

_____

April 14

The Lord gave, and the Lord hath taken away; blessed be the name of the Lord.

Job 1:21 (KJV)

People I am remembering this week:

_____

_____

_____

April 15

The steps of a good man are ordered by the Lord:
and he delighteth in his way.

Psalm 37:23 (KJV)

How I can claim this blessing today:

_____

_____

_____

April 16

Come to me, all you who are weary and bur-
dened, and I will give you rest.

Matthew 11:28 (NIV)

Today I am praying for:

_____

_____

_____

❧

April 17

Happy are they who never saw me and yet have found faith.

John 20:29 (NEB)

How I can put this verse into action today:

_____

_____

_____

April 18

To all who received him, who believed in his name, he gave power to become children of God.

John 1:12 (RSV)

Things that remind me of God's goodness:

_____

_____

_____

April 19

If anyone does sin, we have Jesus Christ, the righteous, who pleads for us with the Father.

1 John 2:1 (TEV)

Blessings God has given me:

April 20

I have loved thee with an everlasting love.

Jeremiah 31:3 (KJV)

My prayer concerns are:

April 21

All this is from God, who through Christ reconciled us to himself and gave us the ministry of reconciliation.

2 Corinthians 5:18 (RSV)

What this verse means to me:

_____

_____

_____

April 22

The Lord is good, a strong hold in the day of trouble; and he knoweth them that trust in him.

Nahum 1:7 (KJV)

Promises I claim today:

_____

_____

_____

April 23

Who forgiveth all thine iniquities; who healeth all thy diseases.

Psalm 103:3 (KJV)

Who needs my love today:

_____

_____

_____

April 24

The needy shall not alway be forgotten: the expectation of the poor shall not perish for ever.

Psalm 9:18 (KJV)

Things that remind me of God's greatness:

_____

_____

_____

❧

April 25

The lines are fallen unto me in pleasant places; yea, I have a goodly heritage.

Psalm 16:6 (KJV)

Today I thank God for:

_____

_____

_____

April 26

Spiritual exercise is valuable in every way, because it promises life both for now and for the future.

1 Timothy 4:8 (TEV)

People I am remembering today:

_____

_____

_____

April 27

I saw the Lord before me at all times; he is by my right side, so that I will not be troubled.

Acts 2:25 (TEV)

How I can claim this blessing today:

April 28

If the Spirit of him who raised Jesus from the dead is living in you, he who raised Christ from the dead will also give life to your mortal bodies through his Spirit, who lives in you.

Romans 8:11 (NIV)

Today I am praying for:

❧

April 29

. . . Christ Jesus, who has destroyed death and has brought life and immortality to light through the gospel.

2 Timothy 1:10 (NIV)

How I can put this verse into action today:

_____

_____

_____

April 30

Those who receive the abundance of grace and the free gift of righteousness reign in life through the one man Jesus Christ.

Romans 5:17 (RSV)

Things that remind me of God's goodness:

_____

_____

❧

May

Sometimes it is not God who leads us through deep valleys and dark waters. It may be man's ignorance and folly. But even then we can feel His presence, for out of our mistakes God can make something beautiful. It is wonderful what God can do with a broken heart when we give Him all the pieces.

Not only is God's way the best and happiest, it is also within our reach. Many shrink from God's will because of a fear that God will ask them to do more than they can do. There *are* some things we cannot do. But of one thing we can be sure: We can do the will of God. With complete faith and confidence, you can pray, "Thy will be done," because God is a loving Father who knows His children better than they know themselves. He wants our best, but He expects no more.

May 1

Behold, I will pour out my spirit unto you, I will make known my words unto you.

Proverbs 1:23 (KJV)

Blessings God has given me:

_____

_____

May 2

Whoever drinks the water that I will give him will never be thirsty again. The water that I will give him will become in him a spring which will provide him with living water, and give him eternal life.

John 4:14 (TEV)

My prayer concerns are:

_____

_____

❧

May 3

We have not received the spirit of the world but the Spirit who is from God, that we may understand what God has freely given us.

              1 Corinthians 2:12 (NIV)

What this verse means to me:

_____

_____

May 4

You have not seen him, yet you love him; and trusting in him now without seeing him, you are transported with a joy too great for words, while you reap the harvest of your faith, that is, salvation for your souls.

              1 Peter 1:8, 9 (NEB)

Promises I claim today:

_____

_____

❧

May 5

I will rejoice in the Lord, I will joy in the God of my salvation.

Habakkuk 3:18 (KJV)

Who needs my love today:

_____

_____

_____

May 6

I have spoken thus to you, so that my joy may be in you, and your joy complete.

John 15:11 (NEB)

Things that remind me of God's greatness:

_____

_____

_____

May 7

"I am the bread of life," Jesus told them. "He who comes to me will never be hungry; he who believes in me will never be thirsty."

John 6:35 (TEV)

Today I thank God for:

_____

_____

_____

May 8

I will betroth thee unto me for ever; yea, I will betroth thee unto me in righteousness, and in judgment, and in lovingkindness, and in mercies.

Hosea 2:19 (KJV)

People I am remembering this week:

_____

_____

May 9

Never will I leave you; never will I forsake you.
Hebrews 13:5 (NIV)

How I can claim this blessing today:

May 10

Thou art my hope, O Lord God: thou art my trust from my youth.

Psalm 71:5 (KJV)

Today I am praying for:

❦

May 11

In the multitude of my thoughts within me thy comforts delight my soul.

Psalm 94:19 (KJV)

How I can put this verse into action today:

_____

_____

May 12

The joy of the Lord is your strength.

Nehemiah 8:10 (KJV)

Things that remind me of God's goodness:

_____

_____

_____

May 13

Behold, I stand at the door and knock; if any one hears my voice and opens the door, I will come in to him and eat with him, and he with me.

Revelation 3:20 (RSV)

Blessings God has given me:

May 14

I myself will give you power of utterance and a wisdom which no opponent will be able to resist or refute.

Luke 21:15 (NEB)

My prayer concerns are:

❦

May 15

He maketh me to lie down in green pastures: he leadeth me beside the still waters.

Psalm 23:2 (KJV)

What this verse means to me:

_____

_____

_____

May 16

I will have mercy on their transgressions, and will no longer remember their sins.

Hebrews 8:12 (TEV)

Promises I claim today:

_____

_____

_____

❧

May 17

Your faith has saved you; go in peace.

Luke 7:50 (NIV)

Who needs my love today:

_____

_____

_____

_____

May 18

Everything is possible to one who has faith.

Mark 9:23 (NEB)

Things that remind me of God's greatness:

_____

_____

_____

May 19

If you abide in me, and my words abide in you, ask whatever you will, and it shall be done for you.

John 15:7 (RSV)

Today I thank God for:

_____

_____

_____

May 20

The Lord will give strength unto his people; the Lord will bless his people with peace.

Psalm 29:11 (KJV)

People I am remembering this week:

_____

_____

_____

May 21

Peace I leave with you; my own peace I give you.
I do not give it to you as the world does. . . . do
not be afraid.

John 14:27 (TEV)

How I can claim this blessing today:

_____

_____

_____

May 22

The Lord will command his lovingkindness in
the daytime, and in the night his song shall be
with me.

Psalm 42:8 (KJV)

Today I am praying for:

_____

_____

May 23

The Lord thy God in the midst of thee is mighty; he will save, he will rejoice over thee with joy; he will rest in his love, he will joy over thee with singing.

Zephaniah 3:17 (KJV)

How I can put this verse into action today:

_____

_____

_____

May 24

As the bridegroom rejoiceth over the bride, so shall thy God rejoice over thee.

Isaiah 62:5 (KJV)

Things that remind me of God's goodness:

_____

_____

May 25

The Lord will perfect that which concerneth me: thy mercy, O Lord, endureth for ever: forsake not the works of thine own hands.

Psalm 138:8 (KJV)

Blessings God has given me:

_____

_____

_____

May 26

Being confident of this, that he who began a good work in you will carry it on to completion until the day of Christ Jesus.

Philippians 1:6 (NIV)

My prayer concerns are:

_____

_____

❦

May 27

I will establish my covenant between me and thee and thy seed after thee in their generations for an everlasting covenant, to be a God unto thee, and to thy seed after thee.

Genesis 17:7 (KJV)

What this verse means to me:

_____

_____

_____

May 28

And my God will supply all your wants out of the magnificence of his riches in Christ Jesus.

Philippians 4:19 (NEB)

Promises I claim today:

_____

_____

❦

May 29

Lo, I am with you always, to the close of the age.
Matthew 28:20 (RSV)

Who needs my love today:

May 30

After I go and prepare a place for you, I will come back and take you to myself, so that you will be where I am.

John 14:3 (TEV)

Things that remind me of God's greatness:

May 31

What the law was powerless to do . . . God did by sending his own Son in the likeness of sinful man to be a sin offering.

Romans 8:3 (NIV)

Today I thank God for:

_____

_____

_____

_____

❧

❦

June

Study the lives of great people, and you will find every one of them drew apart from the hurry of life for rest and reflection. Great poems are not written on crowded streets, lovely songs are not written in the midst of clamoring multitudes; our visions of God come when we stop.

Elijah found God, not in the earthquake or the fire, but in "a still small voice." Moses saw the burning bush as he was out on the hillside. Jesus took time to be alone and to pray.

This is a difficult thing for us to do. We will work for the Lord, we will sing, preach, teach. We will even suffer and sacrifice. But sometimes we forget that before Jesus sent out His disciples to conquer the world, He told them to tarry for prayer and the power of God. Sometimes God puts us on our backs in order to give us a chance to look up. Many times we are forced, not by God but by circumstances of one sort or another, to lie down. "He maketh me to lie down." That can always be a blessed experience.

❦

June 1

Blessed be the God and Father of our Lord Jesus Christ, the Father of mercies and God of all comfort.

2 Corinthians 1:3 (RSV)

People I am remembering this week:

_____

_____

_____

June 2

Be of good courage, and he shall strengthen your heart, all ye that hope in the Lord.

Psalm 31:24 (KJV)

How I can claim this blessing today:

_____

_____

_____

June 3

The law of the Lord is perfect, converting the soul: the testimony of the Lord is sure, making wise the simple. The statutes of the Lord are right, rejoicing the heart: the commandment of the Lord is pure, enlightening the eyes.

Psalm 19:7, 8 (KJV)

Today I am praying for:

_____

_____

June 4

The sacred writings which have power to make you wise and lead you to salvation through faith in Christ Jesus.

2 Timothy 3:15 (NEB)

How I can put this verse into action today:

_____

_____

June 5

Blessed is the man that walketh not in the counsel of the ungodly, nor standeth in the way of sinners, nor sitteth in the seat of the scornful.

Psalm 1:1 (KJV)

Things that remind me of God's goodness:

—————————————————————

—————————————————————

—————————————————————

June 6

I have told you this so that you will have peace by being united to me. The world will make you suffer. But be brave! I have defeated the world!

John 16:33 (TEV)

Blessings God has given me:

—————————————————————

—————————————————————

❧

June 7

Blessed be the Lord, who daily loadeth us with benefits, even the God of our salvation.

Psalm 68:19 (KJV)

My prayer concerns are:

June 8

The Lord preserveth the simple: I was brought low, and he helped me.

Psalm 116:6 (KJV)

What this verse means to me:

❧

June 9

Thou wilt keep him in perfect peace, whose mind is stayed on thee.... Trust ye in the Lord for ever: for in the Lord Jehovah is everlasting strength.

Isaiah 26:3, 4 (KJV)

Promises I claim today:

_____

_____

_____

June 10

For in this hope we were saved.

Romans 8:24 (NIV)

Who needs my love today:

_____

_____

_____

June 11

The Lord is good unto them that wait for him, to the soul that seeketh him. It is good that a man should both hope and quietly wait for the salvation of the Lord.

Lamentations 3:25, 26 (KJV)

Things that remind me of God's greatness:

_____

_____

_____

June 12

I will lift up mine eyes unto the hills, from whence cometh my help. My help cometh from the Lord, which made heaven and earth.

Psalm 121:1, 2 (KJV)

Today I thank God for:

_____

_____

June 13

The Lord is not slow about his promise as some count slowness, but is forbearing toward you, not wishing that any should perish, but that all should reach repentance.

2 Peter 3:9 (RSV)

People I am remembering this week:

_____

_____

_____

June 14

My grace is all you need; power comes to its full strength in weakness.

2 Corinthians 12:9 (NEB)

How I can claim this blessing today:

_____

_____

June 15

Whoever declares publicly that he belongs to me, I will do the same for him before my Father in heaven.

Matthew 10:32 (TEV)

Today I am praying for:

_____

_____

June 16

If my people, which are called by my name, shall humble themselves, and pray, and seek my face, and turn from their wicked ways; then will I hear from heaven, and will forgive their sin, and will heal their land.

2 Chronicles 7:14 (KJV)

How I can put this verse into action today:

_____

_____

June 17

Let the wicked forsake his way, and the unrighteous man his thoughts: and let him return unto the Lord, and he will have mercy upon him; and to our God, for he will abundantly pardon.

Isaiah 55:7 (KJV)

Things that remind me of God's goodness:

_____

_____

_____

June 18

I tell you the truth, my Father will give you whatever you ask in my name.

John 16:23 (NIV)

Blessings God has given me:

_____

_____

June 19

And we receive from him whatever we ask, because we keep his commandments and do what pleases him.

1 John 3:22 (RSV)

My prayer concerns are:

June 20

But if that is how God clothes the grass, which is growing in the field today, and tomorrow is thrown on the stove, how much more will he clothe you! How little faith you have!

Luke 12:28 (NEB)

What this verse means to me:

❧

June 21

As far as the east is from the west, so far hath he removed our transgressions from us.

Psalm 103:12 (KJV)

Promises I claim today:

_____

_____

_____

June 22

Though your sins be as scarlet, they shall be as white as snow; though they be red like crimson, they shall be as wool.

Isaiah 1:18 (KJV)

Who needs my love today:

_____

_____

_____

June 23

[He] forgiveth all thine iniquities; [he] healeth all thy diseases.

Psalm 103:3 (KJV)

Things that remind me of God's greatness:

_____

_____

_____

June 24

Thou, Lord, wilt bless the righteous; with favour wilt thou compass him as with a shield.

Psalm 5:12 (KJV)

Today I thank God for:

_____

_____

_____

June 25

He that followeth after righteousness and mercy findeth life, righteousness, and honour.

Proverbs 21:21 (KJV)

People I am remembering this week:

_____

_____

_____

June 26

Surely goodness and mercy shall follow me all the days of my life: and I will dwell in the house of the Lord for ever.

Psalm 23:6 (KJV)

How I can claim this blessing today:

_____

_____

_____

❧

June 27

Thou wilt shew me the path of life: in thy presence is fulness of joy; at thy right hand there are pleasures for evermore.

Psalm 16:11 (KJV)

Today I am praying for:

_____

_____

June 28

Therefore the redeemed of the Lord shall return, and come with singing unto Zion; and everlasting joy shall be upon their head: they shall obtain gladness and joy; and sorrow and mourning shall flee away.

Isaiah 51:11 (KJV)

How I can put this verse into action today:

_____

_____

June 29

The Lord is good, a strong hold in the day of trouble; and he knoweth them that trust in him.

Nahum 1:7 (KJV)

Things that remind me of God's goodness:

_____

_____

_____

June 30

But you are the chosen race, the King's priests, the holy nation, God's own people, chosen to proclaim the wonderful acts of God, who called you from the darkness into his own marvelous light.

1 Peter 2:9 (TEV)

Blessings God has given me:

_____

_____

❦

July

Sometimes we want God's blessings without the pain of God's purging. We want sermons on how to win friends, how to have peace of mind, and how to forget our fears. But we must remember that Christ came to make men good rather than merely to make them feel good.

Maybe you are afraid. You dread to come into His presence. You are ashamed to face Him. You may feel miserable inside. Then take heart and be glad, for your very shame and misery and fear are a mourning that can lead you to His comfort.

As you look at your life you may see your own broken heart. Be glad that it is broken. Take it to Calvary. There, under the warm glow of His love, your broken heart can be welded together again, and your sorrow be turned into rejoicing. Be thankful for your broken heart, if by becoming broken you are led to Christ for the mending.

❦

July 1

The work of righteousness shall be peace; and the effect of righteousness quietness and assurance for ever.

Isaiah 32:17 (KJV)

My prayer concerns are:

_____

_____

July 2

May our Lord Jesus Christ himself and God our Father, who loved us and by his grace gave us eternal encouragement and good hope, encourage your hearts and strengthen you in every good deed and word.

2 Thessalonians 2:16, 17 (NIV)

What this verse means to me:

_____

_____

🐦

July 3

Mark the perfect man, and behold the upright:
for the end of that man is peace.

Psalm 37:37 (KJV)

Promises I claim today:

_____

_____

_____

July 4

For this God is our God for ever and ever: he will
be our guide even unto death.

Psalm 48:14 (KJV)

Who needs my love today:

_____

_____

_____

❧

July 5

My flesh and my heart faileth: but God is the strength of my heart, and my portion for ever.
Psalm 73:26 (KJV)

Things that remind me of God's greatness:

_____

_____

_____

July 6

The Lord . . . forsaketh not his saints; they are preserved for ever.
Psalm 37:28 (KJV)

Today I thank God for:

_____

_____

_____

❦

July 7

For unto us a child is born, unto us a son is given: and the government shall be upon his shoulder: and his name shall be called Wonderful, Counsellor, The mighty God, The everlasting Father, The Prince of Peace.

                                    Isaiah 9:6 (KJV)

People I am remembering this week:

_____

_____

July 8

Everyone whom my Father gives me will come to me. I will never turn away anyone who comes to me.

                                    John 6:37 (TEV)

How I can claim this blessing today:

_____

_____

❦

July 9

Ye shall go out with joy, and be led forth with peace.

Isaiah 55:12 (KJV)

Today I am praying for:

_____

_____

_____

July 10

Let the righteous be glad; let them rejoice before God: yea, let them exceedingly rejoice.

Psalm 68:3 (KJV)

How I can put this verse into action today:

_____

_____

_____

July 11

The righteous shall be glad in the Lord, and shall trust in him; and all the upright in heart shall glory.

Psalm 64:10 (KJV)

Things that remind me of God's goodness:

_____

_____

_____

July 12

And now these three remain: faith, hope and love. But the greatest of these is love.

1 Corinthians 13:13 (NIV)

Blessings God has given me:

_____

_____

_____

❧

July 13

The Lord shall open unto thee his good treasure, the heaven to give the rain unto thy land in his season, and to bless all the work of thine hand.

Deuteronomy 28:12 (KJV)

My prayer concerns are:

July 14

Love bears all things . . . endures all things.

1 Corinthians 13:7 (RSV)

What this verse means to me:

❧

July 15

I am the resurrection and I am life. If a man has faith in me, even though he die, he shall come to life.

John 11:25 (NEB)

Promises I claim today:

July 16

He will wipe away all tears from their eyes. There will be no more death, no more grief, crying, or pain. The old things have disappeared.

Revelation 21:4 (TEV)

Who needs my love today:

❧

July 17

And, behold, I am with thee, and will keep thee in all places whither thou goest.

Genesis 28:15 (KJV)

Things that remind me of God's greatness:

_____

_____

_____

July 18

How beautiful upon the mountains are the feet of him that bringeth good tidings, that publisheth peace; that bringeth good tidings of good, that publisheth salvation; that saith unto Zion, Thy God reigneth!

Isaiah 52:7 (KJV)

Today I thank God for:

_____

_____

❦

July 19

A new command I give you: Love one another. As I have loved you, so you must love one another.

John 13:34 (NIV)

People I am remembering this week:

_____

_____

_____

July 20

Because thy lovingkindness is better than life, my lips shall praise thee. Thus will I bless thee while I live: I will lift up my hands in thy name.

Psalm 63:3, 4 (KJV)

How I can claim this blessing today:

_____

_____

❧

July 21

... Who crowneth thee with lovingkindness and tender mercies.

Psalm 103:4 (KJV)

Today I am praying for:

_____

_____

_____

July 22

Walk in love, as Christ loved us and gave himself up for us, a fragrant offering and sacrifice to God.

Ephesians 5:2 (RSV)

How I can put this verse into action today:

_____

_____

_____

❧

July 23

My present bodily life is lived by faith in the Son of God, who loved me and gave himself up for me.

Galatians 2:20 (NEB)

Things that remind me of God's goodness:

_____

_____

_____

July 24

They shall be my people, and I will be their God: for they shall return unto me with their whole heart.

Jeremiah 24:7 (KJV)

Blessings God has given me:

_____

_____

July 25

Turn thou me, and I shall be turned; for thou art
the Lord my God.

Jeremiah 31:18 (KJV)

My prayer concerns are:

July 26

It was not because of any good works that we
ourselves had done, but because of his own
mercy that he saved us.

Titus 3:5 (TEV)

What this verse means to me:

❧

July 27

The mountains shall depart, and the hills be removed; but my kindness shall not depart from thee, neither shall the covenant of my peace be removed, saith the Lord that hath mercy on thee.

Isaiah 54:10 (KJV)

Promises I claim today:

July 28

Resting on the hope of eternal life, which God, who does not lie, promised before the beginning of time.

Titus 1:2 (NIV)

Who needs my love today:

❧

July 29

He has granted to us his precious and very great promises.

2 Peter 1:4 (RSV)

Things that remind me of God's greatness:

_____

_____

_____

_____

July 30

If God is on our side, who is against us?

Romans 8:31 (NEB)

Today I thank God for:

_____

_____

_____

July 31

The Lord takes thought for me. Thou art my help and my deliverer; do not tarry, O my God.
Psalm 40:17 (RSV)

People I am remembering this week:

_____

_____

_____

❧

❧

August

We come to the forks of life's road and cannot decide which way to turn. There are decisions to be made, and yet it is so hard to decide. We do get lost. We need guidance. Confidently, David, in the Twenty-third Psalm, declares, "He leadeth me in the paths of righteousness" (in the right paths).

Though God does not promise us an easy, effortless life, He does promise us strength and He does promise to go with us. Notice that the psalm says, "He leadeth me." God doesn't drive. He is climbing the same hill that we climb—man is not alone. As we take life one step at a time, we can walk with Him in the right paths.

❧

August 1

Store up treasure in heaven, where there is no moth and no rust to spoil it, no thieves to break in and steal. For where your treasure is, there will your heart be also.

Matthew 6:20, 21 (NEB)

How I can claim this blessing today:

_____

_____

_____

August 2

This is the day which the Lord hath made; we will rejoice and be glad in it.

Psalm 118:24 (KJV)

Today I am praying for:

_____

_____

❧

August 3

The Lord thy God, he it is that doth go with thee; he will not fail thee, nor forsake thee.

Deuteronomy 31:6 (KJV)

How I can put this verse into action today:

_____

_____

_____

August 4

Train up a child in the way he should go: and when he is old, he will not depart from it.

Proverbs 22:6 (KJV)

Things that remind me of God's goodness:

_____

_____

_____

August 5

Christ will make his home in your hearts, through faith.

Ephesians 3:17 (TEV)

Blessings God has given me:

_____

_____

_____

August 6

And the bow shall be in the cloud; and I will look upon it, that I may remember the everlasting covenant between God and every living creature of all flesh that is upon the earth.

Genesis 9:16 (KJV)

My prayer concerns are:

_____

_____

❧

August 7

The price of wisdom is above rubies.

Job 28:18 (KJV)

What this verse means to me:

_____

_____

_____

August 8

As the heaven is high above the earth, so great is his mercy toward them that fear him.

Psalm 103:11 (KJV)

Promises I claim today:

_____

_____

_____

_____

August 9

Them that honour me, I will honour.

1 Samuel 2:30 (KJV)

Who needs my love today:

_____

_____

_____

August 10

For thou, Lord, art good, and ready to forgive;
and plenteous in mercy unto all them that call
upon thee.... In the day of my trouble I will call
upon thee: for thou wilt answer me.

Psalm 86:5, 7 (KJV)

Things that remind me of God's greatness:

_____

_____

_____

August 11

He satisfieth the longing soul, and filleth the hungry soul with goodness.

Psalm 107:9 (KJV)

Today I thank God for:

_____

_____

August 12

Man does not live on bread alone, but on every word that comes from the mouth of God.

Matthew 4:4 (NIV)

People I am remembering this week:

_____

_____

_____

August 13

He preserveth the souls of his saints; he delivereth them out of the hand of the wicked.

Psalm 97:10 (KJV)

How I can claim this blessing today:

_____

_____

_____

August 14

If we confess our sins, he is faithful and just, and will forgive our sins and cleanse us from all unrighteousness.

1 John 1:9 (RSV)

Today I am praying for:

_____

_____

_____

❧

August 15

Depart from evil, and do good; and dwell for evermore.

Psalm 37:27 (KJV)

How I can put this verse into action today:

_____

_____

_____

August 16

Be ye strong therefore, and let not your hands be weak: for your work shall be rewarded.

2 Chronicles 15:7 (KJV)

Things that remind me of God's goodness:

_____

_____

_____

❧

August 17

If we live, we live for the Lord; and if we die, we die for the Lord. Whether therefore we live or die, we belong to the Lord.

Romans 14:8 (NEB)

Blessings God has given me:

_____

_____

_____

August 18

The Lord preserveth the faithful.

Psalm 31:23 (KJV)

My prayer concerns are:

_____

_____

_____

August 19

The righteous shall flourish like the palm tree:
he shall grow like a cedar in Lebanon.

Psalm 92:12 (KJV)

What this verse means to me:

_____

_____

_____

August 20

If any of you lacks wisdom, he should pray to
God, who will give it to him; because God gives
generously and graciously to all.

James 1:5 (TEV)

Promises I claim today:

_____

_____

_____

❦

August 21

For where two or three come together in my name, there am I with them.

Matthew 18:20 (NIV)

Who needs my love today:

_____

_____

_____

August 22

God is faithful, and he will not let you be tempted beyond your strength, but with the temptation will also provide the way of escape, that you may be able to endure it.

1 Corinthians 10:13 (RSV)

Things that remind me of God's greatness:

_____

_____

August 23

The Spirit of God joins with our spirit in testifying that we are God's children.

Romans 8:16 (NEB)

Today I thank God for:

_____

_____

_____

August 24

Your light must shine before people, so that they will see the good things you do and give praise to your Father in heaven.

Matthew 5:16 (TEV)

People I am remembering this week:

_____

_____

_____

❦

August 25

And hope does not disappoint us, because God has poured out his love into our hearts by the Holy Spirit, whom he has given us.

Romans 5:5 (NIV)

How I can claim this blessing today:

_____

_____

_____

August 26

We look not to the things that are seen but to the things that are unseen; for the things that are seen are transient, but the things that are unseen are eternal.

2 Corinthians 4:18 (RSV)

Today I am praying for:

_____

_____

❧

August 27

They that be wise shall shine as the brightness of the firmament; and they that turn many to righteousness as the stars for ever and ever.

Daniel 12:3 (KJV)

How I can put this verse into action today:

_____

_____

_____

August 28

Have no fear, little flock; for your Father has chosen to give you the Kingdom.

Luke 12:32 (NEB)

Things that remind me of God's goodness:

_____

_____

_____

August 29

Then Jesus said to the woman, "Your sins are forgiven. . . . Your faith has saved you; go in peace."

Luke 7:48, 50 (TEV)

Blessings God has given me:

_____

_____

_____

August 30

The Lord is my light and my salvation; whom shall I fear? the Lord is the strength of my life; of whom shall I be afraid?

Psalm 27:1 (KJV)

My prayer concerns are:

_____

_____

August 31

Our help is in the name of the Lord, who made heaven and earth.

Psalm 124:8 (KJV)

What this verse means to me:

_____

_____

_____

❧

❦

September

We come to those dark places in life through which we are compelled to pass. Death is one. Disappointment is another. Loneliness is another. There are many more.

I have told many people in "the valley of the shadow" to go off by themselves to a quiet place. Quit struggling for a little while. Forget the many details. Stop your mind for a little while from hurrying on to the morrow and to next year and beyond.

Just stop, become still and quiet, and in the midst of your "glen of gloom" you will feel a strange and marvelous presence more powerfully than you have ever felt it before. Many have told me of feeling that presence—of hearing the nightingale sing in the darkness.

"I will not be afraid," said David. Why? There is power in His presence.

❦

September 1

Though outwardly we are wasting away, yet inwardly we are being renewed day by day.

2 Corinthians 4:16 (NIV)

Promises I claim today:

_____

_____

_____

September 2

I know whom I have believed, and I am sure that he is able to guard until that Day what has been entrusted to me.

2 Timothy 1:12 (RSV)

Who needs my love today:

_____

_____

_____

September 3

Yea, though I walk through the valley of the shadow of death, I will fear no evil: for thou art with me; thy rod and thy staff they comfort me.
                                          Psalm 23:4 (KJV)

Things that remind me of God's greatness:

_____

_____

_____

September 4

I will ask the Father, and he will give you another to be your Advocate, who will be with you for ever. . . . I will not leave you bereft; I am coming back to you.

                              John 14:16, 18 (NEB)

Today I thank God for:

_____

_____

❧

September 5

God's Kingdom is not a matter of eating and drinking, but of the righteousness, peace, and joy that the Holy Spirit gives.

Romans 14:17 (TEV)

People I am remembering this week:

_____

_____

_____

September 6

He shall give his angels charge over thee, to keep thee in all thy ways. They shall bear thee up in their hands, lest thou dash thy foot against a stone.

Psalm 91:11, 12 (KJV)

How I can claim this blessing today:

_____

_____

September 7

My soul shall be satisfied as with marrow and fatness; and my mouth shall praise thee with joyful lips.

Psalm 63:5 (KJV)

Today I am praying for:

_____

_____

_____

September 8

The voice of rejoicing and salvation is in the tabernacles of the righteous.

Psalm 118:15 (KJV)

How I can put this verse into action today:

_____

_____

_____

❧

September 9

Light is sown for the righteous, and gladness for the upright in heart.

Psalm 97:11 (KJV)

Things that remind me of God's goodness:

_____

_____

_____

September 10

"Believe in the Lord Jesus," they said, "and you will be saved—you and your family."

Acts 16:31 (TEV)

Blessings God has given me:

_____

_____

_____

September 11

"Let the little children come to me, and do not hinder them, for the kingdom of God belongs to such as these." . . . And he took the children in his arms, put his hands on them and blessed them.

Mark 10:14, 16 (NIV)

My prayer concerns are:

_____

_____

_____

September 12

He is a buckler to all those that trust in him.

Psalm 18:30 (KJV)

What this verse means to me:

_____

_____

❧

September 13

He who is faithful in a very little is faithful also in much.

Luke 16:10 (RSV)

Promises I claim today:

_____

_____

_____

September 14

In all thy ways acknowledge him, and he shall direct thy paths.

Proverbs 3:6 (KJV)

Who needs my love today:

_____

_____

_____

September 15

Cast thy burden upon the Lord, and he shall sustain thee: he shall never suffer the righteous to be moved.

Psalm 55:22 (KJV)

Things that remind me of God's greatness:

_____

_____

_____

September 16

But courage! The victory is mine; I have conquered the world.

John 16:33 (NEB)

Today I thank God for:

_____

_____

_____

September 17

Every child of God is able to defeat the world. This is how we win the victory over the world: with our faith.

1 John 5:4 (TEV)

People I am remembering this week:

_____

_____

_____

September 18

Behold, God is my salvation; I will trust, and not be afraid: for the Lord Jehovah is my strength and my song; he also is become my salvation.

Isaiah 12:2 (KJV)

How I can claim this blessing today:

_____

_____

❧

September 19

Now may the Lord of peace himself give you peace at all times and in every way.

2 Thessalonians 3:16 (NIV)

Today I am praying for:

_____

_____

_____

September 20

I waited patiently for the Lord; and he inclined unto me, and heard my cry.

Psalm 40:1 (KJV)

How I can put this verse into action today:

_____

_____

_____

❧

September 21

They that trust in the Lord shall be as mount Zion, which cannot be removed, but abideth for ever.

Psalm 125:1 (KJV)

Things that remind me of God's goodness:

_____

_____

September 22

Who saved us and called us with a holy calling, not in virtue of our works but in virtue of his own purpose and the grace which He gave us in Christ Jesus ages ago.

2 Timothy 1:9 (RSV)

Blessings God has given me:

_____

_____

❦

September 23

Behold, how good and how pleasant it is for brethren to dwell together in unity!

Psalm 133:1 (KJV)

My prayer concerns are:

_____

_____

_____

September 24

For it is by his grace you are saved, through trusting him; it is not your own doing. It is God's gift.

Ephesians 2:8 (NEB)

What this verse means to me:

_____

_____

_____

September 25

For thou, Lord, art good, and ready to forgive; and plenteous in mercy unto all them that call upon thee.

Psalm 86:5 (KJV)

Promises I claim today:

_____

_____

September 26

So there is no difference between Jews and Gentiles, between slaves and free men, between men and women; you are all one in union with Christ Jesus.

Galatians 3:28 (TEV)

Who needs my love today:

_____

_____

September 27

For through him we both have access to the Father by one Spirit.

Ephesians 2:18 (NIV)

Things that remind me of God's greatness:

_____

_____

_____

September 28

See what love the Father has given us, that we should be called children of God; and so we are.

1 John 3:1 (RSV)

Today I thank God for:

_____

_____

_____

September 29

What we have seen and heard we declare to you, so that you and we together may share in a common life, that life which we share with the Father and his Son Jesus Christ.

1 John 1:3 (NEB)

People I am remembering this week:

_____

_____

_____

September 30

Know that the Lord hath set apart him that is godly for himself: the Lord will hear when I call unto him.

Psalm 4:3 (KJV)

How I can claim this blessing today:

_____

_____

❦

October

The lives of those we call saints, those who have attained unusual spiritual power, teach us an important secret. They sinned, but they never surrendered to sin. They never accepted failure as final. They never ceased to look forward with confidence. They kept saying, "I can in Him." And to the utmost of their power was added His power.

The same power is available for any one of us. You may look into a past of shame and defeat, but I tell you that you can look into a future of peace and victory. "Only believe, only believe all things are possible, only believe." That is more than just a little chorus. It is the Christian faith.

❦

October 1

If you have love for one another, then all will know that you are my disciples.

John 13:35 (TEV)

Today I am praying for:

_____

_____

_____

October 2

Blessed are the peacemakers, for they will be called sons of God.

Matthew 5:9 (NIV)

How I can put this verse into action today:

_____

_____

_____

October 3

He that hath mercy on the poor, happy is he.
Proverbs 14:21 (KJV)
Things that remind me of God's goodness:

_____

_____

_____

October 4

I came that they may have life, and have it abundantly.

John 10:10 (RSV)

Blessings God has given me:

_____

_____

_____

_____

October 5

Truly, I say to you, unless you turn and become like children, you will never enter the kingdom of heaven. Whoever humbles himself like this child, he is the greatest in the kingdom of heaven.

Matthew 18:3, 4 (RSV)

My prayer concerns are:

_____

_____

October 6

Let us therefore boldly approach the throne of our gracious God, where we may receive mercy and in his grace find timely help.

Hebrews 4:16 (NEB)

What this verse means to me:

_____

_____

October 7

Come near to God, and he will come near to you.
James 4:8 (TEV)

Promises I claim today:

_____

_____

_____

October 8

Yet the Lord will command his lovingkindness
in the daytime, and in the night his song shall be
with me, and my prayer unto the God of my life.
Psalm 42:8 (KJV)

Who needs my love today:

_____

_____

_____

🍂

October 9

When you pray, go into your room, close the door and pray to your Father, who is unseen. Then your Father, who sees what is done in secret, will reward you.

Matthew 6:6 (NIV)

Things that remind me of God's greatness:

_____

_____

_____

October 10

When a man's ways please the Lord, he maketh even his enemies to be at peace with him.

Proverbs 16:7 (KJV)

Today I thank God for:

_____

_____

❧

October 11

He shall send from heaven, and save me from
the reproach of him that would swallow me up
... God shall send forth his mercy and his truth.

Psalm 57:3 (KJV)

People I am remembering this week:

_____

_____

_____

October 12

Hearken unto me, ye that know righteousness,
the people in whose heart is my law; fear ye not
the reproach of men, neither be ye afraid of their
revilings.

Isaiah 51:7 (KJV)

How I can claim this blessing today:

_____

_____

❧

October 13

If they obey and serve him, they shall spend their days in prosperity, and their years in pleasures.

Job 36:11 (KJV)

Today I am praying for:

_____

_____

_____

October 14

He who does the will of God abides for ever.
1 John 2:17 (RSV)

How I can put this verse into action today:

_____

_____

_____

❧

October 15

Whoever does the will of my heavenly Father is
my brother, my sister, my mother.

Matthew 12:50 (NEB)

Things that remind me of God's goodness:

_____

_____

_____

October 16

And ye shall serve the Lord your God, and he
shall bless thy bread, and thy water.

Exodus 23:25 (KJV)

Blessings God has given me:

_____

_____

_____

❦

October 17

Thou shalt keep therefore his statutes . . . that it may go well with thee, and with thy children after thee.

Deuteronomy 4:40 (KJV)

My prayer concerns are:

_____

_____

_____

October 18

Every man should eat and drink, and enjoy the good of all his labour, it is the gift of God.

Ecclesiastes 3:13 (KJV)

What this verse means to me:

_____

_____

_____

October 19

There is nothing in all creation that will ever be able to separate us from the love of God which is ours through Christ Jesus our Lord.

Romans 8:39 (TEV)

Promises I claim today:

_____

_____

_____

October 20

The mercy of the Lord is from everlasting to everlasting upon them that fear him.

Psalm 103:17 (KJV)

Who needs my love today:

_____

_____

_____

October 21

Humble yourselves, therefore, under God's mighty hand, that he may lift you up in due time. Cast all your anxiety on him because he cares for you.

1 Peter 5:6, 7 (NIV)

Things that remind me of God's greatness:

_____

_____

_____

October 22

For by grace you have been saved through faith; and this is not your own doing, it is the gift of God.

Ephesians 2:8 (RSV)

Today I thank God for:

_____

_____

❦

October 23

The light of the righteous rejoiceth. . . . to the righteous good shall be repaid.

Proverbs 13:9, 21 (KJV)

People I am remembering this week:

_____

_____

_____

October 24

The Lord is my shepherd; I shall not want. . . . Thou preparest a table before me in the presence of mine enemies: thou anointest my head with oil; my cup runneth over.

Psalm 23:1, 5 (KJV)

How I can claim this blessing today:

_____

_____

❧

October 25

The Lord will rescue me from every attempt to do me harm, and keep me safe until his heavenly reign begins.

2 Timothy 4:18 (NEB)

Today I am praying for:

_____

_____

_____

October 26

You that are blessed by my Father: come! Come and receive the kingdom which has been prepared for you ever since the creation of the world.

Matthew 25:34 (TEV)

How I can put this verse into action today:

_____

_____

October 27

He that is slow to anger is better than the mighty; and he that ruleth his spirit than he that taketh a city.

Proverbs 16:32 (KJV)

Things that remind me of God's goodness:

_____

_____

_____

October 28

For everyone who exalts himself will be humbled, and he who humbles himself will be exalted.

Luke 14:11 (NIV)

Blessings God has given me:

_____

_____

❧

October 29

In the house of the righteous is much treasure.
Proverbs 15:6 (KJV)

My prayer concerns are:

_____

_____

_____

October 30

For God did not give us a spirit of timidity but a spirit of power and love and self-control.
2 Timothy 1:7 (RSV)

What this verse means to me:

_____

_____

_____

_____

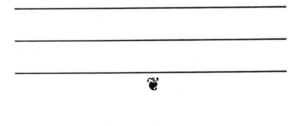

October 31

So that everyone who believes in him may have
eternal life.

John 3:15 (TEV)

Promises I claim today:

_____

_____

_____

🌿

November

"Blessed are the poor in spirit; for theirs is the kingdom of heaven." The "poor in spirit" have so emptied themselves of themselves—the pride of their accomplishments, the selfishness of their desires—that the Spirit of God has come into their emptiness.

Someone has said, "All that religion has to offer is self-denial in this life on the promise of some pie in the sky." But notice that Jesus uses the verb "is." His Kingdom becomes an immediate possession. It is not a place, it is an experience. It is not bounded by geographical lines, it is bounded only by our capacity to receive it.

In the light of the blessings of possessing the Kingdom of God, all our other possessions grow so dim that out of our very hearts we sing: "When other helpers fail, and comforts flee, help of the helpless, O abide with me."

November 1

God did not appoint us to suffer wrath but to receive salvation through our Lord Jesus Christ.

1 Thessalonians 5:9 (NIV)

Who needs my love today:

_____

_____

November 2

Thou shalt guide me with thy counsel, and afterward receive me to glory.

Psalm 73:24 (KJV)

Things that remind me of God's greatness:

_____

_____

_____

November 3

Lord, thou wilt ordain peace for us.

Isaiah 26:12 (KJV)

Today I thank God for:

_____

_____

_____

November 4

I will both lay me down in peace, and sleep: for thou, Lord, only makest me dwell in safety.

Psalm 4:8 (KJV)

People I am remembering this week:

_____

_____

_____

_____

November 5

My grace is all you need; power comes to its full strength in weakness.

2 Corinthians 12:9 (NEB)

How I can claim this blessing today:

November 6

Then shalt thou have thy delight in the Almighty, and shalt lift up thy face unto God.

Job 22:26 (KJV)

Today I am praying for:

November 7

For thou hast been a shelter for me, and a strong tower from the enemy.

Psalm 61:3 (KJV)

How I can put this verse into action today:

November 8

So let us never tire of doing good, for if we do not slacken our efforts we shall in due time reap our harvest.

Galatians 6:9 (NEB)

Things that remind me of God's goodness:

November 9

I am thy shield, and thy exceeding great reward.
Genesis 15:1 (KJV)

Blessings God has given me:

_____

_____

_____

November 10

The eternal God is thy refuge, and underneath
are the everlasting arms.
Deuteronomy 33:27 (KJV)

My prayer concerns are:

_____

_____

_____

_____

November 11

My presence shall go with thee, and I will give thee rest.

Exodus 33:14 (KJV)

What this verse means to me:

_____

_____

_____

November 12

As the mountains are round about Jerusalem, so the Lord is round about his people from hence-forth even for ever.

Psalm 125:2 (KJV)

Promises I claim today:

_____

_____

_____

❧

November 13

When thou liest down, thou shalt not be afraid:
yea, thou shalt lie down, and thy sleep shall be
sweet.

Proverbs 3:24 (KJV)

Who needs my love today:

November 14

He giveth power to the faint; and to them that
have no might he increaseth strength.

Isaiah 40:29 (KJV)

Things that remind me of God's greatness:

November 15

The God who said, "Out of darkness the light shall shine!" is the same God who made his light shine in our hearts, to bring us the light of the knowledge of God's glory.

2 Corinthians 4:6 (TEV)

Today I thank God for:

November 16

The Son of God has come and has given us understanding, so that we may know him who is true. And we are in him who is true—even in his Son Jesus Christ.

1 John 5:20 (NIV)

People I am remembering this week:

❧

November 17

Again Jesus spoke to them, saying, "I am the light of the world; he who follows me will not walk in darkness, but will have the light of life."

John 8:12 (RSV)

How I can claim this blessing today:

_____

_____

November 18

Let us even exult in our present sufferings, because we know that suffering trains us to endure, and endurance brings proof that we have stood the test, and this proof is the ground of hope.

Romans 5:3, 4 (NEB)

Today I am praying for:

_____

_____

❦

November 19

He healeth the broken in heart, and bindeth up their wounds.

Psalm 147:3 (KJV)

How I can put this verse into action today:

November 20

So then, my dear brothers, stand firm and steady. Keep busy always in your work for the Lord, since you know that nothing you do in the Lord's service is ever without value.

1 Corinthians 15:58 (TEV)

Things that remind me of God's goodness:

❧

November 21

Call upon me in the day of trouble: I will deliver thee, and thou shalt glorify me.

Psalm 50:15 (KJV)

Blessings God has given me:

_____

_____

_____

November 22

O thou that hearest prayer, unto thee shall all flesh come.

Psalm 65:2 (KJV)

My prayer concerns are:

_____

_____

_____

November 23

He will be very gracious unto thee at the voice
of thy cry; when he shall hear it, he will answer
thee.

Isaiah 30:19 (KJV)

What this verse means to me:

_____

_____

_____

November 24

Thou shalt make thy prayer unto him, and he
shall hear thee.

Job 22:27 (KJV)

Promises I claim today:

_____

_____

_____

❧

November 25

I will do whatever you ask in my name, so that the Son may bring glory to the Father. You may ask me for anything in my name, and I will do it.

John 14:13, 14 (NIV)

Who needs my love today:

_____

_____

_____

November 26

And this is the confidence which we have in him, that if we ask anything according to his will he hears us.

1 John 5:14 (RSV)

Things that remind me of God's greatness:

_____

_____

❧

November 27

His love was disclosed to us in this, that he sent his only Son into the world to bring us life.

1 John 4:9 (NEB)

Today I thank God for:

_____

_____

_____

November 28

God is love, and whoever lives in love lives in God and God lives in him.

1 John 4:16 (TEV)

People I am remembering this week:

_____

_____

_____

November 29

I will praise thee; for I am fearfully and wonderfully made: marvelous are thy works; and that my soul knoweth right well.

Psalm 139:14 (KJV)

How I can claim this blessing today:

_____

_____

November 30

Whatever is true, whatever is noble, whatever is right, whatever is pure, whatever is lovely, whatever is admirable—if anything is excellent or praiseworthy—think about such things.

Philippians 4:8 (NIV)

Today I am praying for:

_____

_____

❧

December

The angel climaxed the announcement of the birth of our Lord with the words, "Glory to God in the highest, and on earth peace, good will toward men" (Luke 2:14 KJV). Peace was His mission. "Peace I leave with you, my peace I give unto you" (John 14:27 KJV). When we think of the Kingdom of God, we think of a kingdom of peace, where all strife has ceased. So we are not surprised that our Lord gave peace as one of the keys to the Kingdom.

What is peace? The mere absence of strife is not peace. Peace is a positive force. To have peace in both the world and our souls, not only must hate, suspicion, and fear be rooted out. Love, joy, patience, and understanding must also be planted and cultivated. Peace is something to be made; thus we must be peacemakers if we are to enter the Kingdom of God.

December 1

Give, and it will be given to you; good measure, pressed down, shaken together, running over, will be put into your lap. For the measure you give will be the measure you get back.

Luke 6:38 (RSV)

How I can put this verse into action today:

December 2

Remember: sparse sowing, sparse reaping; sow bountifully, and you will reap bountifully. . . . God loves a cheerful giver.

2 Corinthians 9:6, 7 (NEB)

Things that remind me of God's goodness:

December 3

Let us give thanks to the God and Father of our Lord Jesus Christ: For he has blessed us, in our union with Christ, by giving us every spiritual gift in the heavenly world.

Ephesians 1:3 (TEV)

Blessings God has given me:

December 4

All the paths of the Lord are mercy and truth unto such as keep his covenant and his testimonies.

Psalm 25:10 (KJV)

My prayer concerns are:

December 5

And are justified freely by his grace through the redemption that came by Christ Jesus.

Romans 3:24 (NIV)

What this verse means to me:

December 6

I am the Alpha and the Omega, the beginning and the end. To the thirsty I will give from the fountain of the water of life without payment.

Revelation 21:6 (RSV)

Promises I claim today:

❦

December 7

How blest are those who hunger and thirst to see right prevail; they shall be satisfied.

Matthew 5:6 (NEB)

Who needs my love today:

_____

_____

December 8

Take my yoke and put it on you, and learn from me, because I am gentle and humble in spirit; and you will find rest.

Matthew 11:29 (TEV)

Things that remind me of God's greatness:

_____

_____

December 9

Yet shall ye be as the wings of a dove covered
with silver, and her feathers with yellow gold.

Psalm 68:13 (KJV)

Today I thank God for:

_____

_____

_____

December 10

For I know the plans I have for you, says the
Lord, plans for welfare and not for evil, to give
you a future and a hope.

Jeremiah 29:11 (RSV)

People I am remembering this week:

_____

_____

_____

❧

December 11

The path of the just is as the shining light, that shineth more and more unto the perfect day.

Proverbs 4:18 (KJV)

How I can claim this blessing today:

_____

_____

_____

December 12

Not everyone who says to me, "Lord, Lord," will enter the kingdom of heaven, but only he who does the will of my Father who is in heaven.

Matthew 7:21 (NIV)

Today I am praying for:

_____

_____

_____

December 13

He that keepeth the law, happy is he.
Proverbs 29:18 (KJV)

How I can put this verse into action today:

_____

_____

_____

December 14

The lessons I taught you, the tradition I have passed on, all that you heard me say or saw me do, put into practice; and the God of peace will be with you.
Philippians 4:9 (NEB)

Things that remind me of God's goodness:

_____

_____

_____

December 15

By me thy days shall be multiplied, and the years of thy life shall be increased.

Proverbs 9:11 (KJV)

Blessings God has given me:

_____

_____

_____

December 16

The beloved of the Lord shall dwell in safety by him; and the Lord shall cover him all the day long.

Deuteronomy 33:12 (KJV)

My prayer concerns are:

_____

_____

_____

❧

December 17

They that wait upon the Lord shall renew their strength; they shall mount up with wings as eagles; they shall run, and not be weary; and they shall walk, and not faint.

Isaiah 40:31 (KJV)

What this verse means to me:

_____

_____

_____

December 18

God loved the world so much that he gave his only Son, that everyone who has faith in him may not die but have eternal life.

John 3:16 (NEB)

Promises I claim today:

_____

_____

December 19

Because I live, you also will live.

John 14:19 (TEV)

Who needs my love today:

_____

_____

_____

December 20

And the peace of God, which transcends all understanding, will guard your hearts and your minds in Christ Jesus.

Philippians 4:7 (NIV)

Things that remind me of God's greatness:

_____

_____

_____

❧

December 21

Rejoice and be glad, for your reward is great in heaven.

Matthew 5:12 (RSV)

Today I thank God for:

_____

_____

_____

December 22

Have I not commanded thee? Be strong and of a good courage; be not afraid, neither be thou dismayed: for the Lord thy God is with thee whithersoever thou goest.

Joshua 1:9 (KJV)

People I am remembering this week:

_____

_____

December 23

O bless our God, ye people, and make the voice of his praise to be heard: which holdeth our soul in life, and suffereth not our feet to be moved.

Psalm 66:8, 9 (KJV)

How I can claim this blessing today:

December 24

With thee is the fountain of life: in thy light shall we see light.

Psalm 36:9 (KJV)

Today I am praying for:

❦

December 25

Today in the city of David a deliverer has been born to you—the Messiah, the Lord.

Luke 2:11 (NEB)

How I can put this verse into action today:

_____

_____

_____

December 26

We are often troubled, but not crushed; sometimes in doubt, but never in despair; there are many enemies, but we are never without a friend; and though badly hurt at times, we are not destroyed.

2 Corinthians 4:8, 9 (TEV)

Things that remind me of God's goodness:

_____

_____

❧

December 27

Forgive as the Lord forgave you.

Colossians 3:13 (NIV)

Blessings God has given me:

_____

_____

_____

December 28

For the mountains shall depart, and the hills be removed; but my kindness shall not depart from thee, neither shall the covenant of my peace be removed, saith the Lord that hath mercy on thee.

Isaiah 54:10 (KJV)

My prayer concerns are:

_____

_____

_____

❧

December 29

Unto him that is able to keep you from falling,
and to present you faultless before the presence
of his glory with exceeding joy.

Jude 24 (KJV)

What this verse means to me:

_____

_____

_____

December 30

I will greatly rejoice in the Lord, my soul shall
be joyful in my God.

Isaiah 61:10 (KJV)

Promises I claim today:

_____

_____

_____

December 31

Therefore, since we are justified by faith, we have peace with God through our Lord Jesus Christ. Through him we have obtained access to this grace in which we stand, and we rejoice in our hope of sharing the glory of God.

Romans 5:1, 2 (RSV)

Who needs my love today:

_____

_____

_____